DK eyewonder

Cars

LONDON, NEW YORK,
MELBOURNE, MUNICH, and DELHI

DK UK
Written and edited by Caroline Stamps
Art editor Clare Marshall
Jacket editor Manisha Majithia
Jacket designer Mark Cavanagh
Jacket design development manager
Sophia M Tampakopoulos Turner
Producer (print production) Mary Slater
Producer (pre-production) Rachel Ng
Publisher Andrew Macintyre
Consultant Giles Chapman

DK INDIA
Senior editor Shatarupa Chaudhuri
Senior art editor Rajnish Kashyap
Assistant editors Priyanka Kharbanda,
Neha Chaudhary
Art editors Nishesh Batnagar, Pooja Pawwar
Managing editor Alka Thakur Hazarika
Managing art editor Romi Chakraborty
Pre-production manager Balwant Singh
DTP designer Dheeraj Singh
Picture researcher Sumedha Chopra

First published in Great Britain in 2014 by
Dorling Kindersley Limited
80 Strand, London WC2R 0RL

Copyright © 2014 Dorling Kindersley Limited
A Penguin Company

13 14 15 16 17 10 9 8 7 6 5 4 3 2 1
001 – 196177 – 02/14

A CIP catalogue record for this book
is available from the British Library.

ISBN 978-1-4093-383

Colour reproduction by Scanhouse, Malaysia
Printed and bound in China by

Discover more at
www.dk.com

Contents

4-5
The first cars

6-7
Types of car

8-9
How is a car made?

10-11
Formula 1

12-13
Rallying

14-15
NASCAR

16-17
Monster trucks

18-19
Dragster

20-21
Go-karting!

22-23
Stay safe

24-25
Long and short

26-27
Supercars

28-29
Fame!

30-31
Speed demons

32-33
Car tower

34-35
Just an idea...

36-37
Speedy stunts

38-39
Cars in space

40-41
We need fuel

42-43
Start to finish

44-45
Weird and wonderful

46-47
True or false?

48-49
Get set, go...

50-51
What's this?

52-53
Which way?

54-55
Glossary

56
Index and
acknowledgements

The first cars

We depend on cars to carry us from place to place and millions are in use on our roads. The first cars looked very different from those we see today, and borrowed heavily from bicycles and carriages in their design.

Look, four wheels!
In 1886, Gottlieb Daimler and Wilhelm Maybach fitted an engine onto a stagecoach. This was the first four-wheeled petrol-engined vehicle.

The first car
The three-wheeled Benz Motorwagen, designed by Karl Benz in 1885, looked like a cross between a carriage and a bicycle.

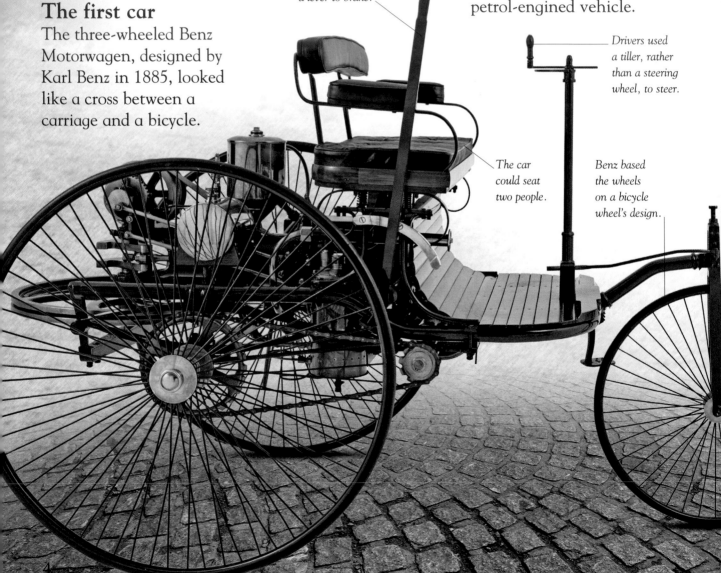

The driver used a lever to brake.

Drivers used a tiller, rather than a steering wheel, to steer.

The car could seat two people.

Benz based the wheels on a bicycle wheel's design.

Speeding up production

With a growing market, car production needed to speed up. The Ford Model T was the first car to be built on a moving assembly line, which was introduced by Henry Ford in 1913. To speed up the process, from 1914 until 1926 most Model Ts were painted in black as the enamel dried faster than other colours.

From its arrival in 1908 till the end of its production in 1927, more than 15 million Ford Model Ts were made.

RED FLAG ACT

Before cars appeared, a British law (The Locomotive Act 1865) was passed, banning a self-propelled vehicle from travelling at more than 6 kph (4 mph), while a man had to walk ahead of the vehicle with a red flag. These restrictions were lifted in 1896.

The hood could be folded back.

Brass-framed windscreen

Built by hand

In 1913, a Ford Model T took just 93 minutes to build. By 1914, an impressive 1,000 cars were rolling off the production line each day. All assembly was by hand.

Wire wheels replaced wooden ones in 1926.

Moving on

In the 1920s, car ownership became more common and more affordable, and manufacturers competed for a growing market. Small cars, such as the Austin Seven, were especially popular.

Types of car

Look around you. A huge variety of cars are on our roads. They range in size, shape, and power. Yet, there is a small number of basic types of car. These are some of the ones you will probably see.

I win!
The next time you go for an outing, play a game with a friend. Identify the types of car on the road and see who spots the most types.

Hatchback
A hatchback has three or five doors, with the third or fifth door at the back, and rear seats that fold to increase luggage space.

Sports car
A low-slung two-door sports car will have a powerful engine. The first sports car, the Vauxhall 30-98, came out in 1913.

The Dodge Viper SRT10 has a top speed of 332 kph (206 mph).

The boot opens to reveal luggage space.

Saloon

This is a good-sized car for a family. A saloon has four doors, as well as an enclosed boot.

The roof can be folded back at the touch of a button.

Convertible

These cars have a roof that folds back in seconds, making them ideal for sunny days.

MPVs are taller than saloons and hatchbacks.

MPV

A Multi-Purpose Vehicle (MPV) is a popular choice for larger families, as it has more seats than a regular family car. Many have seven seats.

SUV

Sport-Utility Vehicles (SUVs) are large cars with excellent suspension and four-wheel drive. This means they can cope with off-road conditions.

How is a car made?

The first cars were built by hand, but once production lines began, faster processes were put in place. In the 1970s, robots made an appearance. Here's a peek at a car factory.

Turn it this way!

The skeleton car bodies hang from a moving galley, so workers can easily access each car's panel.

The swings are designed to turn the cars around.

Robotic care

The car's body, including the roof, is welded in place by robots. Once ready, each car's body is given a unique vehicle identification number (VIN).

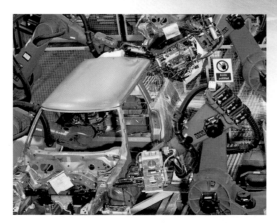

Ready for fitting

In this factory, the newly painted cars sit in a revolving swing, ready for the parts (such as the engine, the headlights, and the radiator) to be added.

Fitting the parts

The "guts" of the car – the engine and gear box – are pushed up into the car's frame from below by robots, then bolted in place.

Each car has been spray-painted and dried in a drying room.

Nearly done!

The car is almost ready for its final inspection, with finishing touches, such as the wheels, being added by hand.

Formula 1

A Grand Prix race sees powerful Formula 1 (F1) racing cars screaming around a track at speeds of 340 kph (211 mph). A race lasts about 90 minutes, during which time the cars cover some 300 km (186 miles). An F1 race is fast and furious.

Clever steering
An F1 steering wheel can contain more than 100 working parts. The driver has paddles on the wheel for changing the gears.

A lightweight machine
The F1 teams construct their own cars following set specifications. It takes a few thousand components to make an F1 car. However, despite the number of parts, the cars are surprisingly light in weight.

Monaco Grand Prix

First held in 1929, this exciting race sees cars complete 78 laps through narrow, twisting city streets. This is one of the most famous hairpin bends the drivers have to tackle.

Pit stop

When a driver makes a pit stop, the crew members change the four wheels and tyres, refuel the car, and clean the driver's visor – all in just six seconds.

Change those tyres!

F1 tyres are built to last less than one race. There are different tyres for different weather conditions.

Intermediate tread tyres are used on wet tracks, with no standing water.

Slick tyres have no tread. They are used for dry conditions.

Heavy tread tyres are used on tracks with standing water. They move the water out of the way, for better grip.

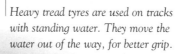

F1 flags

During an F1 race, different flags are used to "talk" to the drivers.

A green flag means that warnings issued earlier in the race are now cleared.

A red flag indicates that the race has been stopped and all drivers must pull in.

This striped flag warns drivers of a wet track, which may be due to water or oil.

The chequered flag is shown first to the winner and signals the end of the race.

Rallying

Off-road endurance racing is fast and furious, with the cars following a planned route that takes them over all sorts of terrain, from rocky ground to flowing water. Some races last one day, while others last several days. The courses are always challenging.

A peep inside

A rally car may look like a road car, but it is very different. It has bucket seats, an enormous fuel tank, and a tough inner cage to protect the two occupants.

The cars are adapted for use on rough ground at high speed.

Going into the air over the brow of a hill is known as hill jumping.

Up and over

During a rally, a car may leave the ground, forced up by the driver accelerating over the brow of a hill. Rally cars take a massive battering in the course of a race.

Dakar

The Dakar Rally, originally held in Europe and Africa, now takes place in South America each year. Hundreds of cars, motorbikes, and trucks start this tough race, but many don't finish. These are specially made for the Dakar race.

The Dakar Rally takes place over 15 days. Huge support vehicles are used to help cars out of trouble.

Accident!

Crashes are common during rallies. Poor weather can flood a course in minutes, making the ground muddy, while boulders on the route can flip a car. In seconds, a car can be wrecked and out of the race.

Sometimes a quick repair is possible – but not always.

Snow, mud, rocks, ice...

Off-road races take place on a variety of ground and the driver has to concentrate on controlling the car. That's why rally drivers have a passenger, who takes charge of navigating the exact route.

NASCAR

NASCAR (which stands for the National Association for Stock Car Auto Racing) is an incredibly popular race series in the USA, with more than 40 cars competing in a lengthy, high-speed chase around a circuit. The first official NASCAR race was held in 1949, in North Carolina, USA.

They're off!

A NASCAR race begins with a rolling start, which means the cars are moving when the race officially begins. The drivers line up their cars behind a pace car and follow it around the track. The pace car reaches 113 kph (70 mph) and then pulls over. The green flag waves, and the drivers race off.

That's a bit too close!

Bumps and crashes are common because the cars are driven so close to each other. Drivers wear crash helmets, and the cars have roll cages – protective inner frames made with steel tubes.

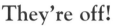
A window net helps to keep the driver safe during a crash.

Fast and furious

They may look a little like road cars, but these cars are high-powered racing machines with about five times the power of a regular family car. They can reach speeds of more than 320 kph (200 mph).

MOONSHINE

NASCAR has its origins in the 1920s, when smugglers of the alcoholic drinks moonshine and whiskey transported their goods in cars that were changed so they were faster than police cars. The drivers became skilled at driving quickly over dirt tracks, and some organized informal races. The first official NASCAR race was held on a beach.

A spectator sport

NASCAR is held at speedway tracks in front of massive crowds of spectators. The largest stadiums can seat more than 150,000 people. The Indianapolis Motor Speedway can accommodate more than 250,000!

Monster trucks

These mighty machines entertain spectators at shows all over the world. They are used for racing, while their big wheels and high axles allow the drivers to take them over a variety of obstacles – often old cars.

Tyres

A large monster truck may have tyres that are 3 m (10 ft) in diameter, although most are smaller. Such tyres were originally taken from farm machinery, and are designed to spread a heavy weight.

All monster trucks have a name.

The raised suspension is designed to absorb shocks and so help the car withstand a high jump.

I'll beat you!

A monster truck show usually sees two trucks racing around a circuit, followed by a freestyle event at which individual trucks roll over obstacles. There are also ramps, which help the trucks bounce up into the air.

A cool disguise

Monster trucks started as converted pickups, but they are now often purpose-built. Many have highly decorated paintwork. All have a strong frame and huge wheels. This truck is known as *The Zombie*. Its "arms" are removed before a show, and its presence certainly draws crowds.

The Zombie at the Monster Jam motosport event

Removable "arms"

Monstrous facts

● A monster truck's tyres are not fully pumped, so they can squash as they roll over an obstacle.

● The first monster truck, called *Bigfoot 1*, was built by Bob Chandler and first shown in 1981.

● Monster trucks crush more than 3,000 unwanted cars each year.

Demolition fun

Vehicles, such as cars and vans, from local scrapyards are used as obstacles for the monster trucks. The full-size vehicles are crushed by the trucks as a demonstration of their power.

Dragster

Two drag cars line up, their back wheels spinning. The starting lights flash green, the cars shoot off, and the air fills with a deafening roar. In less than a second, these dragsters will reach 160 kph (100 mph). A couple more seconds, and the race is over. Blink and you'll have missed it!

These lights flash when the cars stand 17.7 cm (7 in) behind the starting line.

These lights indicate that the cars are at the starting line.

Amber lights flash together as a countdown to the start.

Green lights signal the start of the race.

Red lights flash in case of a foul start.

Christmas tree

An electronic light system, called the Christmas tree, is used as a countdown for the race. If a red light flashes, a driver has pulled away too soon and is disqualified.

Burnout

A dragster's back wheels are spun before a race. This is done to clean them of grit and heat them, which is known as the burnout. It makes the rubber hot and sticky so that the tyres have a better grip. It also causes a lot of smoke! Flames sometimes shoot out as well.

Stop!

A top fuel dragster shoots down a track that is just 305 m (1,000 ft) in length. A roll cage protects the driver. These cars reach such high speeds that parachutes are the best way of stopping them.

Dragster facts

● Dragsters can reach more than 530 kph (330 mph) by the finish line – in just 4.5 seconds!

● Top fuel dragsters race on shorter tracks, but other types of dragster use tracks that are 402 m (1,319 ft) long.

● Noise at a top fuel dragster race reaches dangerous levels – spectators usually wear earplugs.

Driver's kit

Drag racing can be a dangerous sport. The driver sits in front of an engine that packs an explosive punch. Each driver wears a fireproof suit, in addition to thick gloves, a neck brace, and a helmet.

Dragster driver

A long, narrow body helps the car to cut through the air.

The front wing helps to hold the front of the car down.

TIRE KINGDOM

19

Go-karting!

Get ready, watch for the flag, and… go! It's fun to experience the fast-paced excitement of a car race. Young racers can join the action with a go-kart.

A first kart

Toy "cars" without motors have been enjoyed for many years. Karts, such as this one, are usually home-built and depend on a slope to get them moving.

Simple to control

A go-kart has a steering wheel, a brake pedal, and a throttle, which makes the kart speed up. These karts are easy machines to use.

Fun karts

There are many places to try go-karting. Simple circuits will have safety barriers made from old tyres.

Formula 1 legend Michael Schumacher waves to the crowd after a karting race.

An early start

Most F1 racing-car stars, including Michael Schumacher and Lewis Hamilton, began their career by racing go-karts. Schumacher was the European karting champion in 1987.

MOTORIZED SPEED

Motorized go-karts were invented in the USA in the 1950s. They had small engines, and one of the first, in fact, used an adapted chainsaw motor.

A challenging circuit

A go-kart circuit is full of twists and hairpin bends. It teaches a young racer important skills, such as the best cornering line to take, as well as control of the kart.

Stay safe

New car models undergo lots of safety testing, which looks at the car's structure and at the safety of those inside. A key feature of car safety tests is crash test dummies – replicas built to look like people.

A "family" of test dummies

Crash tests

Cars are designed to have a crumple zone, where the impact of a crash is absorbed. Combined with the use of airbags and seatbelts, this improves the chances of the occupants' survival in a crash.

Not such a dummy

Crash test dummies have more than 130 tiny sensors. So when they are used in crash simulations, they feed all sorts of data back to computers, which helps improve car safety.

Car safety tests are carefully monitored.

One result of this test is to show how the car's crumple zone reacts.

Ready to roll

This test is designed both to check that a car does not roll too easily on to its side, and also how far it can support itself without crumpling.

A car flying off a ramp during a roll-over crash test

Air cushion

Airbags inflate rapidly in the event of a crash. They cushion the driver and front seat passenger, protecting them from injuries that might occur if they hit the windscreen or wheel.

BELT UP!

The first cars to have safety belts as a standard fitting were made by Saab in 1958. Other car manufacturers soon followed suit. The three-point belt used today was first designed in 1958 by an engineer at Volvo. In some countries, it is now illegal not to use a belt.

Long and short

From very, very short, to very, very long, some cars grab attention wherever they go because of their unusual size. You may have caught sight of a stretch limousine, but have you ever heard of a P50?

This type of back-in parking is illegal in some countries.

Space for me?

Two-seater Smart micro cars first appeared in the late 1990s. They are so short that they can be reversed up to the pavement and parked between two cars, if that's the only available space.

The car has no reverse gear, but is so light that it can be lifted by hand.

There is just one door, on the car's left side.

Peel P50

This three-wheeled mini car first appeared in 1962. The cars are now being made once again, in a factory in England.

A stretch limousine is the length of two family cars.

Stretch limo
The luxurious saloon was first made around 1928. Early stretch limos (then known as "big-band buses") were often used to move touring music bands.

An inside look
These cars are very comfortable inside, with room to stretch out. There is usually a television, and glasses for drinks. They are party cars!

Stretch that one!
Different cars have received the stretch treatment, including Hummers (which are already big cars).

Hummers were originally adapted from military vehicles known as Humvees.

A Hummer has a high ground clearance compared to other road cars.

Supercars

Supercars are super speedy. All these cars have amazing engines – powerplants that give incredible top speeds. Their mid-mounted engines are positioned behind the driver, helping to stabilize the cars at speed.

Forward-lifting bonnet

The doors open up and forwards.

Sleek shape to cut through the air

Lamborghini Countach

This car first appeared in the 1970s. Its scissor doors were hinged at the front and lifted up – the driver had to be careful where he opened this car.

The car was low to the ground, at just 107 cm (42 in) in height.

The Bugatti has a price tag of more than US$1 million.

Supercar facts

- The Lamborghini Countach can reach 274 kph (170 mph).

- The Ferrari F40 can reach 323 kph (202 mph).

- The McLaren F1 has a top speed of 391 kph (242 mph).

- The Bugatti Veyron Super Sport has a top speed of 431.074 kph (267.85 mph).

Ferrari F40

This two-door car was released in 1987. Its entire rear bodywork lifted so the engine could be easily accessed from three sides.

McLaren F1

This car, dating from the 1990s, could accelerate from 0 to 97 kph (0 to 60 mph) in just three seconds! Unusually, the driver sat in a central position, with room for two passengers.

Keep it light

A lightweight glass was used on the engine cover. It reduced the body weight, which helped the car to go faster.

The rear tyres are the largest ever produced for a road car.

Bugatti Veyron

First appearing in the market in 2005, this is currently the world's fastest production car. The car's power and speed mean it needs 10 radiators to help with its cooling system.

Fame!

Lights, camera, action! From *Chitty Chitty Bang Bang* to Batman's Batmobile, some cars have become famous because of their appearance in films. Some are adapted road cars, others are purpose-built.

The Batpod is steered with the rider's shoulders rather than the hands.

A time traveller

The DeLorean DMC-12 sports car achieved fame through its use as a time machine in the *Back to the Future* series of films.

The Tumbler has a stealth mode, which turns off the car's lights and engine.

Speedy racing

Mach 5 is one of the racing cars in the film *Speed Racer*. It has many special features, such as a "fogger" mode that allows it to stay under water for up to 30 minutes.

Go for the gold!

In the film *The Italian Job*, a group of thieves steal a gold shipment by creating a traffic jam. They use three Mini Coopers, a couple of Jaguars, and a bus, to bring Turin, Italy, to a standstill.

A flying car

Six cars were built for the film *Chitty Chitty Bang Bang*: a main car, and versions including one that could extend wings and "fly".

Batmobile

The superhero Batman drives a custom-made car, the Batmobile. Over time, it has changed from a sports car to a tank-like vehicle, known as the *Tumbler*. The *Tumbler* can also convert itself into the Batpod motorcycle.

Speed demons

The first land-speed record was set in 1898. Later, to achieve more speed, jet or rocket engines were used instead of piston (internal combustion) engines. *ThrustSSC* reached a major milestone when it broke the sound barrier in 1997.

These engines burned 18 litres (4.8 US gallons) of fuel per second.

ThrustSSC's engines

Faster than sound

On 15 October 1997, Andy Green climbed into the tight cockpit of *ThrustSuperSonicCar* (*ThrustSSC*). On that day, *ThrustSSC* became the first land vehicle to break the sound barrier officially. This car still holds the land-speed record.

A new record

On its record-breaking run in 1997, *ThrustSSC* reached 1,227.99 kph (763.035 mph). The record took place in the Black Rock Desert, USA.

ThrustSSC is 16.5 m (54 ft) long and 3.7 m (12 ft) wide.

Speed records

There's a long history of competitive driving, as people have fought to be the fastest of all.

18 December 1898: The first land-speed record was set by Count Gaston de Chasseloup-Laubat, who drove 1 km (0.62 miles) in 57 seconds.

Bluebird body being lowered

3 September 1935: Sir Malcolm Campbell clocked 484.620 kph (301.129 mph) in *Bluebird*.

Railton Mobil Special

The future

The team that developed *ThrustSSC* is currently working on a new car that will aim to travel even faster. This car is named *BloodhoundSSC*. Like *ThrustSSC*, it is shaped to make it as fast as possible.

BloodhoundSSC

Why a desert?

Certain deserts are perfect for land-speed record attempts as they are unpopulated, and have an open, flat surface without trees and plants. These were the tracks left by *ThrustSSC*.

Wings helped keep the car on the ground.

16 September 1947: *Railton Mobil Special* achieved 634.39 kph (394.19 mph) at the Bonneville Salt Flats, USA.

23 October 1970: Gary Gabelich reached 1,014.52 kph (630.389 mph) in *Blue Flame*.

Blue Flame

4 October 1983: *Thrust2* broke the land-speed record at Black Rock Desert, USA, reaching 1,019.4 kph (633.468 mph).

Thrust2

Car tower

The world's largest car factory is located in Germany. Known as Autostadt, which means "car town", this Volkswagen factory produces 3,800 cars a day. Autostadt has an ingenious method of displaying some of those newly made cars to buyers.

A LOOK BACK

As soon as more cars began to appear on the roads, planners started looking for ways around the problem of parking. Vertical car parks were an early solution in busy areas. In some ways, Autostadt's towers are a natural development of this.

That space is mine!

Mechanical parking lifts are now fairly common in some large cities. They date back to the 1930s. This one was a bit like a ferris wheel.

I'll have that one!

Some of the cars at Autostadt leave the production line and travel straight to storage pods. They are then easy to get at if somebody wants to buy one.

On show

The cars at Autostadt are stored in two huge cylindrical towers. Each of the towers has 20 storeys, stands 47 m (154 ft) tall, and holds 400 cars.

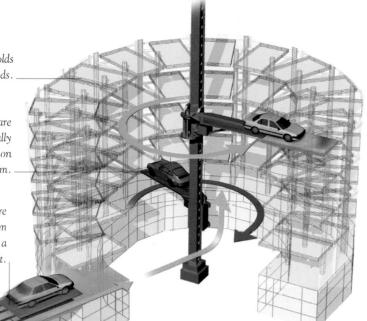

Each storey holds 20 storage pods.

The cars are automatically raised on a platform.

The cars are delivered from the factory on a conveyor belt.

How it works

Each car is moved on a lift, and the lift can move two cars at a time. Cars travel up or down the lift at 7 kph (4.5 mph). The process is computer controlled.

Car towers are a good way of showing off a manufacturer's range of cars.

Just an idea...

Car manufacturers are constantly developing new ideas. Some of these cars are displayed at car shows, and some of the ideas may make it into production. They are known as "concept cars".

Hidden headlamps

Early days

One of the first concept cars, the Buick Y-Job was built in 1938 purely to test new ideas. It had hidden headlights, electric windows, and door handles that didn't stick out.

Bubble canopy

Is it a plane?

General Motors took inspiration from fighter aircraft design to produce the Firebird III, one of a series of three concept cars built in the 1950s.

The rear wheels could tuck forwards.

I'll squeeze in there!

Visitors to the 1992 Paris Motor Show were treated to the sight of a folding car: the Renault Zoom. While parking, the rear wheels could move forwards a little to sit under the car.

A car or a bike?

First presented in 2006, Volkswagen's concept car, the GX3, is often seen as a motorcycle as it has a three-wheel design. It seats two people.

The GX3 has a top speed of 200 kph (125 mph).

The BMW i8's sleek looks won it a place in the film Mission Impossible 4.

The two scissor doors open up and out.

Smooth lines

The BMW i8 concept car is a high-performance sports car, but has an impressive fuel economy of 33 km/l (78 mpg).

Speedy stunts

Cars feature in some amazing stunts to entertain crowds. They also appear in films for action-packed scenes. Let's take a look at a few of these performances.

Move to the left

The Filmka team does film stunts as well as live shows. One of the tricks involves balancing a car so it can be driven on two wheels while a go-kart is driven underneath. One wrong move would spell disaster.

The twin metal loops were 18 m (60 ft) tall.

Finishing touches were given to the tracks before the race.

Double loop track

Get ready, set, go! In 2012, two cars performed in a giant version of a toy-car racing game, taking the loops at a speed of 84 kph (52 mph).

Chase them!

Car-chase scenes in films are packed with action. They often include exciting stunts, such as driving the car down a flight of stairs.

Take off!

Attend a car show and you may see car jumping stunts. This car is jumping over several parked cars, having taken off from a ramp.

Just a movie

It's not unusual for cars to be wrecked in stunts performed for films. They are driven by experienced stunt drivers, and the moves planned in detail to prevent injury.

Cars in space

You can't take any car to the Moon or another planet and expect it to work. Apart from the weight issues of getting it there, there's no oxygen in space, and so the engine wouldn't run. However, special cars, called rovers, have been sent to explore the Moon and Mars.

Destination Mars

In the several unmanned expeditions to Mars, robotic rovers have explored the planet's surface. The rover *Opportunity* has been active since 2004. *Curiosity* landed on Mars in 2012. It is looking for signs of past life and trying to find out if the planet could support life in the future.

A panoramic camera sits on top of the rover's main mast.

An artist's impression of the Curiosity rover

Hop on!

The last three missions to the Moon (Apollo 15, 16, and 17) carried a battery-powered Lunar Roving Vehicle (LRV), or "moon buggy". The LRV could move at a top speed of 18.5 kph (11.5 mph).

Each wheel is 81 cm (32 in) in diameter and has its own electric motor.

Trials on Earth

Lunar rovers need extensive testing on Earth. This one has 12 wheels, and is designed to house two astronauts for extended missions away from their mother ship, without the need to wear spacesuits.

The arm, or Instrument Deployment Device, carries powerful scientific equipment.

How big are they?

Mars' rovers have varied in size. Shown here is the back-up for the first rover, *Sojourner* (front). To the left is a test rover, used on the *Opportunity* programme. The large test rover (right) is the size of *Curiosity*.

We need fuel

Cars need an energy source to make them go, just like you need food. Most cars on our roads use petrol or diesel, but cars running on alternative energy sources are beginning to appear.

It runs on corn

Manufacturers are looking at biofuels, which are fuels made from plants. There are two types of biofuel: ethanol, an alcohol, usually made from corn, and biodiesel, made from vegetable oils, fats, and greases blended with diesel.

The Aurora 101 can seat just one person.

Where's the Sun?

A solar-powered car runs on energy from sunlight. In order to achieve this, it has to be light in weight. This means solar-powered cars cannot meet today's safety or passenger needs.

LIFEcar stands for LIghtweight Fuel Efficient Car.

Hydrogen cell

These cars are powered by hydrogen and can generate their own electricity. The Morgan LIFEcar is a prototype at the moment, but a road version may be developed.

The petrol engine recharges the electric engine's batteries (on which the car sometimes runs), saving fuel and cutting exhaust emissions.

A bit of both

Hybrid cars run on a mix of petrol and electricity. They have an electric motor and a petrol engine.

The Toyota Yaris Hybrid

The car is plugged into a standing point to recharge.

Plug it in

An electric car runs on electricity, and so it needs a regular recharge from a charging point. These cars, therefore, can only travel restricted distances between charges.

Start to finish

Once the shiny new cars leave their factories, how do you think they reach the car showroom? And what happens at the end of their lives? Let's look at the beginning and end of a car's life.

By train

Cars travel in special carriages, called auto racks, which can carry between 12 and 20 vehicles. A train may haul up to 70 of these carriages.

On the road

Cars are distributed by road in car transporters, which usually hold up to 10 cars, on two (or sometimes three) levels.

By ship

Many cars are carried overseas. A huge container ship might hold 8,000 cars. The largest container ship, *Triple E*, holds 18,000 containers, which could altogether house 36,000 cars!

Goodbye, car!

When a vehicle is beyond repair, it is sent to the scrapyard. Despite looking a mess, such cars may have parts that can be recycled.

The doors have already been removed for scrap value.

So that they take up less room, cars are crushed before they are taken to a recycling plant.

Crush it!

Many countries have recycling rules so that a car isn't just crushed and put into a landfill.

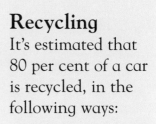

Recycling

It's estimated that 80 per cent of a car is recycled, in the following ways:

Fluids, such as antifreeze and oil, are removed and sent to recycling plants.

The undamaged parts are often sold off to be recycled (in the case of batteries) or reused.

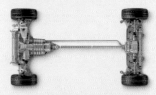

An old car's chassis is usually sent to be melted down for the metal.

The engine is either reconditioned, or the metal may be recycled.

Weird and wonderful

A car is a vehicle that has four wheels, and can take you from A to B along a road. Right? Well, some cars push the boundaries of what a car is.

The Moller is planned as a VTOL (vertical take-off and landing) car.

A flying car?

People have imagined a cross between a car and an aeroplane for many years. The Moller M400 is being developed as a possible flying car, a "skycar".

Amphibious vehicle

Cars that can travel on land and water are rare, but they do exist. The only such car produced for sale to the public was the Amphicar. However, now there are new designs, including this watercar.

The Python watercar can reach up to 96 kph (60 mph) on the water and 201 kph (125 mph) on land.

A fancy look

The VW Beetle has been one of the most popular family cars ever produced. This unusual version has a wrought-ironwork body.

More than 21 million Beetles have been made.

Luggage can be stored under the front bonnet.

Hot rod

These date back to the late 1930s, with cars being beefed up to go faster, and given eye-catching paintwork. Hot rods are still very popular in certain countries.

Hot rods are often highly decorated.

We sell shoes!

Cars are often decorated for advertising purposes or for special events. This electric car in the shape of a giant shoe was made by a footwear manufacturer in China.

The body is made from leather.

True or false?

It's time to test your knowledge about cars. See if you can spot what is true and what is false in this mini quiz.

An F1 car's **steering wheel** has 1,000 working parts.
See page 10

Monster trucks crush more than 50,000 unwanted cars each year.
See page 17

Six cars were built for the film *Chitty Chitty Bang Bang*.
See page 29

An **SUV** has a roof that folds back.
See page 7

Many F1 racing car drivers first competed in **go-karts**.
See page 20

Blue Flame broke the sound barrier in 1997.
See page 31

The **Peel P50** is so light that it can be lifted by hand.
See page 24

The **Filmka team** performs stunts for films as well as live shows.
See page 36

The **Christmas tree light system** is used for the NASCAR race.
See page 18

Hot rods date back to the late 1930s.
See page 45

Car transporters can usually hold up to 50 cars.
See page 42

Get set, go...

Experience the thrill of racing as you drive your car to be the first to reach the finish line... but watch out for hazards on the way.

Crowd cheers you on. **Move forward 4**

Take the corner line. **Move forward 4**

Overtake another car. **Move forward 4**

Burst tyre! **Miss a go**

Poor track. **Go back 3**

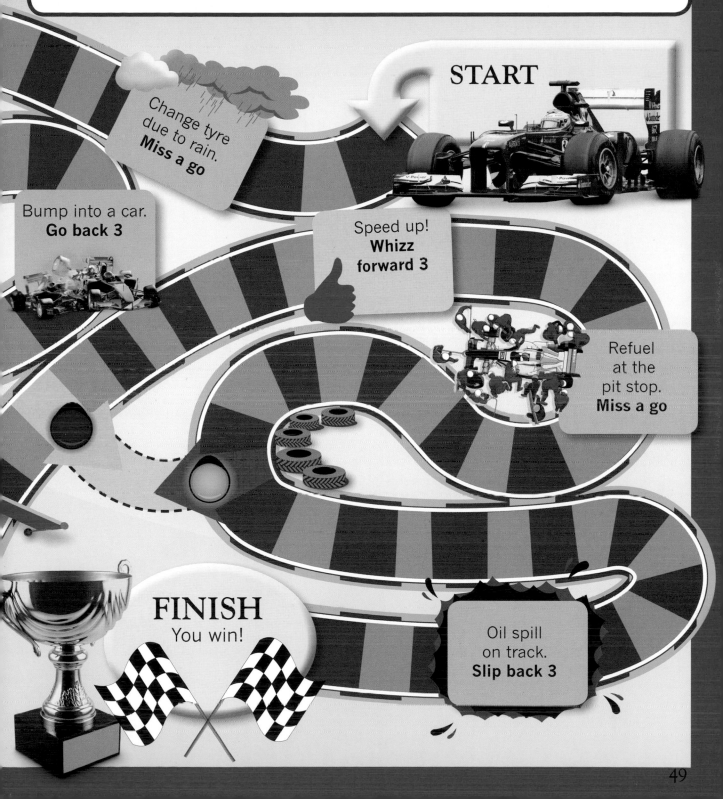

How to play

This game is for up to four players.

You will need
- A dice
- Counters – one for each player.

Move down   **Move up**

Trace over the car outlines, or cut and colour your own from card. Each player takes turns to throw the dice, and begins from the START box. Follow the squares with each roll of the dice. If you land on an instruction, make sure you do as it says. Good luck!

START

Change tyre due to rain. **Miss a go**

Bump into a car. **Go back 3**

Speed up! **Whizz forward 3**

Refuel at the pit stop. **Miss a go**

FINISH You win!

Oil spill on track. **Slip back 3**

What's this?

Take a look at these close-ups of things in the book, and see if you can identify them. The clues should help you!

🚗 These cars are good for sunny days.

🚗 Their roofs can be folded back very quickly.

See page 7

🚗 These cars are ideal for young racers.

🚗 They have throttles that are used to speed up the cars.

See page 20

🚗 These are long, luxurious cars.

🚗 These party cars are comfortable inside.

See page 25

🚗 These high-powered racing cars look like road cars.

🚗 They have window nets to keep the drivers safe.

See page 14

🚗 These vehicles can have tyres as big as 3 m (10 ft) in diameter.

🚗 They are used to perform freestyle stunts.

See page 16

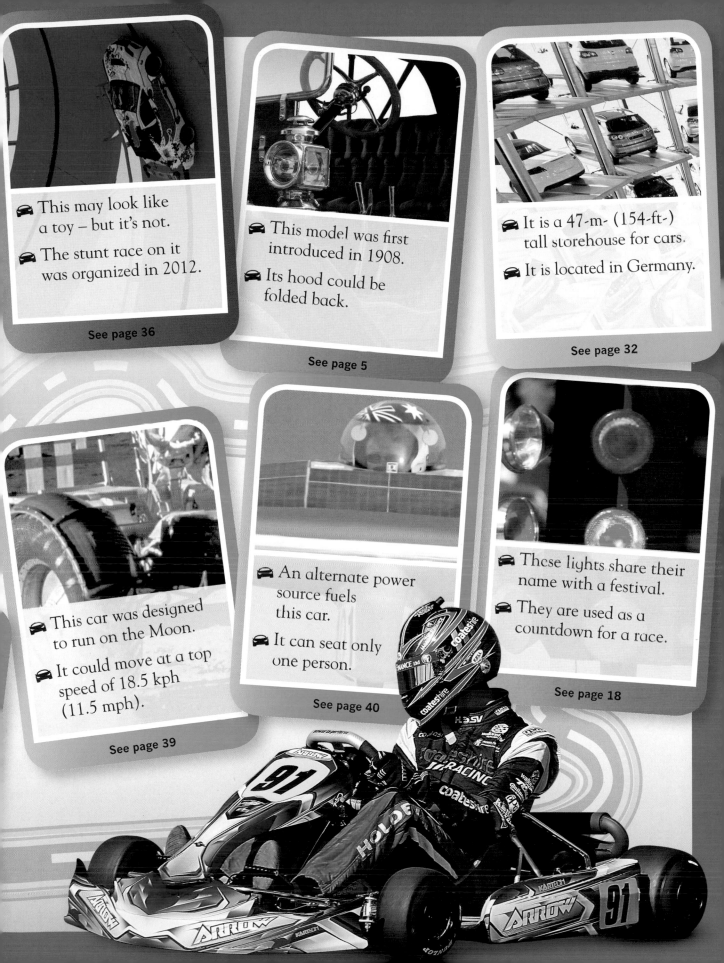

🚗 This may look like a toy – but it's not.

🚗 The stunt race on it was organized in 2012.

See page 36

🚗 This model was first introduced in 1908.

🚗 Its hood could be folded back.

See page 5

🚗 It is a 47-m- (154-ft-) tall storehouse for cars.

🚗 It is located in Germany.

See page 32

🚗 This car was designed to run on the Moon.

🚗 It could move at a top speed of 18.5 kph (11.5 mph).

See page 39

🚗 An alternate power source fuels this car.

🚗 It can seat only one person.

See page 40

🚗 These lights share their name with a festival.

🚗 They are used as a countdown for a race.

See page 18

Which way?

Help the rally car team find a safe route to the finish line. Answer each question correctly to clock the speediest time.

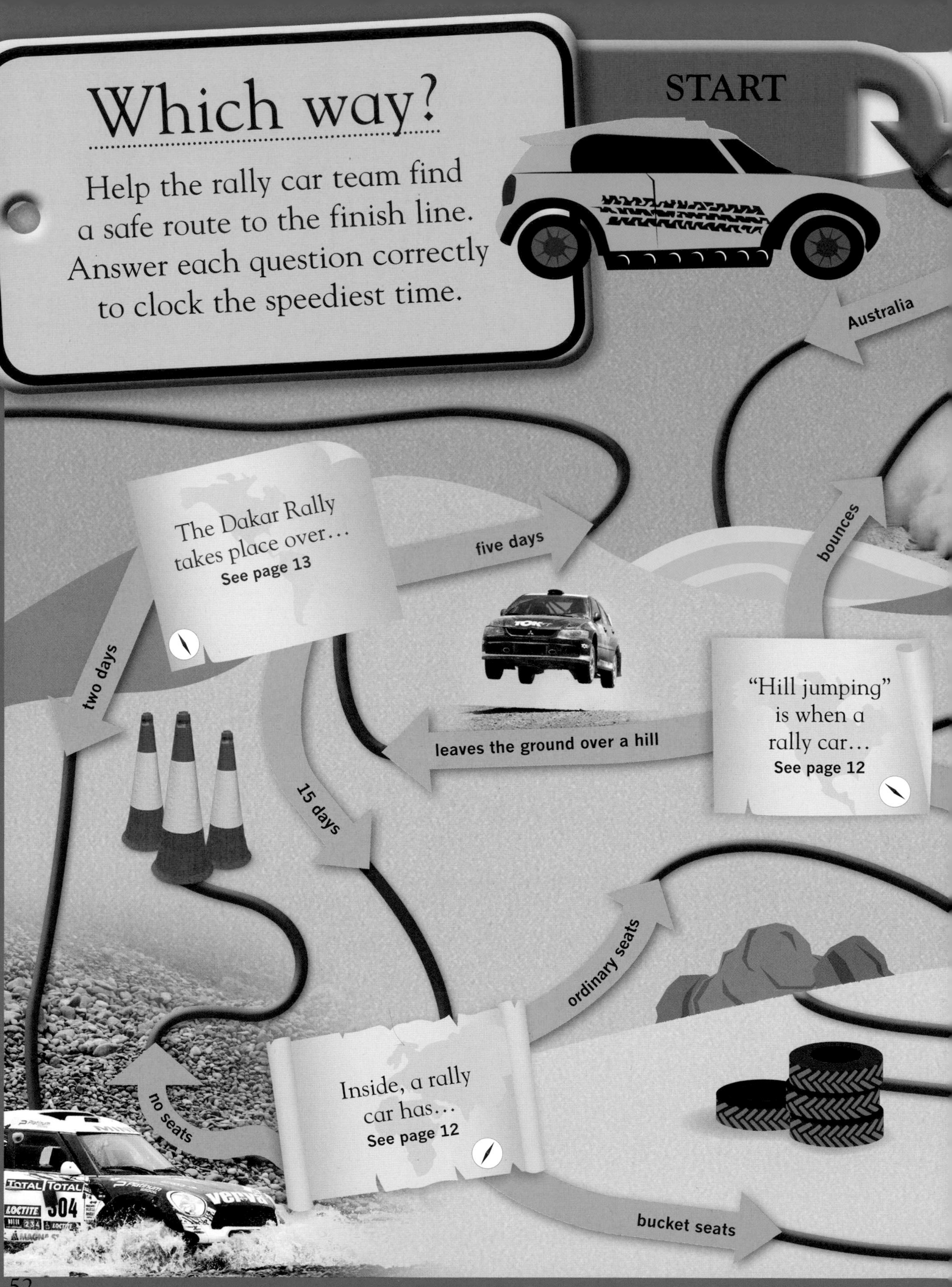

START

Australia

bounces

The Dakar Rally takes place over…
See page 13

five days

two days

"Hill jumping" is when a rally car…
See page 12

leaves the ground over a hill

15 days

ordinary seats

Inside, a rally car has…
See page 12

no seats

bucket seats

52

The Dakar Rally takes place each year in…
See page 13

South America

no passengers

Asia

A rally driver has…
See page 13

three passengers

a navigator

off-road

Rally races take place…
See page 12

on roads

bounces from hill to hill

in indoor circuits

FINISH

Glossary

Here are the meanings of some words that are
useful to know when learning about cars.

Acceleration to speed
up and go faster.

Airbag a safety device
in cars, made of flexible
fabric. In a crash, it inflates
instantly to cushion the driver
and front passenger.

Axle the rod that connects
two wheels, on which the
wheels turn.

Biofuel fuel obtained
from living material. It
is a cleaner and cheaper
alternative to petrol
and diesel.

Carriage a four-wheeled
vehicle pulled by horses.

Chassis a car's basic frame. The
working parts and the car's body
are attached to the chassis.

Crumple zone the front and
rear portions of a car that
collapse to absorb the impact
in a collision, helping to
protect the passenger area.

Diesel a type of fuel made from
refined oil and used in many
truck and car engines.

Dirt track an unpaved road
race track.

Dragster a powerful racing car,
usually long and narrow,
modified or built for drag racing.

Ethanol a biofuel made by
fermenting sugar and starch.

Formula 1 (F1) a worldwide motor-racing championship featuring very fast, single-seater, open-wheel cars.

Four-wheel drive a system in a vehicle where power from the engine can turn all four wheels.

Fuel economy the amount of fuel used by a car for the distance it travels.

Gears toothed wheels that are used to change the speed or force with which car engines turn.

Go-kart a small, lightweight racing car without a roof.

Grand Prix race an important car or motorcycle race. F1 races are called Grand Prix.

Ground clearance the distance between the ground and the underside of a car.

Hairpin bend a U-shaped bend on a road or track.

Hybrid vehicle a vehicle that has both a petrol engine and another power unit, such as an electric motor.

Internal combustion engine an engine that produces power by burning fuel with air inside a cylinder.

MPV a Multi-Purpose Vehicle, also known as a "people-carrier".

NASCAR National Association for Stock Car Auto Racing, a family-owned organization that authorizes more than 1,500 races.

Navigator a passenger who helps the driver to stick to the route for a vehicle such as a rally car.

Pace car a safety car in a race that leads the race cars and limits their speed before the race is allowed to begin.

Piston a rod-shaped engine part that moves up and down inside a cylinder in an internal combustion engine.

Pit stop a safe area for a racing car to pull over during a race for refuelling, repairs, and a tyre change.

Radiator a device that uses water or another liquid to help cool a vehicle's engine.

Rally a type of race held on public or private roads, in which participants drive between set points. This race does not take place on a circuit.

Recycle to process materials so that they can be reused.

Roll cage a metal structure built into a car's roof (or above the passengers of an open-top car) to prevent or reduce injury if the car tips onto its roof.

Self-propelled vehicle a vehicle that moves by its own power source, such as an engine, rather than being driven by an external force, such as horses.

Sensor a small device that receives signals from the surrounding environment and responds accordingly.

Stagecoach a covered, horse-drawn vehicle, used for transporting passengers.

Suspension a system of springs or shock absorbers that helps a vehicle travel smoothly over bumps and dips, not only making the ride more comfortable for passengers but also helping to protect the car itself.

SUV Sport-Utility Vehicle, a four-wheel drive car with high ground-clearance and spacious bodywork.

Top fuel dragster a dragster that runs on high-energy fuels, such as nitromethane and methanol, instead of petrol or diesel.

Tread the indented pattern on a tyre's surface that provides the grip between the wheels of a vehicle and the ground.

Vehicle identification number (VIN) a unique code stamped on every vehicle by the automobile industry to identify individual motor vehicles.

Index

Airbags 23, 54
Apollo missions 38, 39
Austin Seven 5
Autostadt 32-33

Benz, Karl 4
Bigfoot 1 16, 17
biofuel 40, 54
BloodhoundSSC 31
BMW i8 35
Bugatti Veyron 26-27
Buick Y-Job 34
burnout 18

car transporters 42
Christmas tree 18
concept cars 34-35
convertible 7
crash test dummy 22
crumple zone 22

Daimler, Gottlieb 4
Dakar Rally 13
Dodge Viper SRT10 6
dragster 18-19, 54

electric cars 41

factory 8-9, 32
Ferrari F40 27
Firebird III 34
flags 11
Ford, Henry 5
Ford Model T 5
Formula 1 10-11,
    55
fuel 40-41

go-kart 20-21, 55
Grand Prix racing 10-11,
    55

Hamilton, Lewis 20
hatchback 6
hot rod 45
Hummer 25
hybrid cars 41, 55
hydrogen-cell cars 40

Lamborghini
    Countach 26
land-speed records 30-31
Lunar Roving Vehicle 39

Mars rovers 38, 39
Maybach, Wilhelm 4
McLaren F1 27
Monaco Grand Prix 11
monster truck 16-17
moon rover *see* Lunar
    Roving Vehicle
Morgan LIFEcar 40
Motorwagen 4
MPV (Multi-Purpose
    Vehicle) 7

NASCAR 14-15, 55

off-road racing 12-13

parachute 19
Peel P50 24
pit stop 11, 55

rally racing 12-13, 55
recycling 43, 55
robots 8, 9
roll-over crash test 23

safety 22-23
safety belts 23
saloon 7
Schumacher, Michael 20
Smart car 24
solar power 40
space 38-39
speedway 15
sports car 6
steering wheel 10
stretch limousine 25
stunts 36-37
supercars 26-27
SUV (Sports-Utility
    Vehicle) 7, 55

ThrustSSC 30-31
trains 42
tyres 11

VIN (vehicle identification
    number) 8, 55
Volkswagen GX3 35
VTOL car 44
VW Beetle 45

Watercar 44

Acknowledgements

Dorling Kindersley would like to thank Andy Cooke for artwork and Lorrie Mack for proof reading.

Picture credits

"No U-turn" sign

Dodge Viper

Car key

Mini Cooper S

Classic car

Hatchback

Car covered in grass

Mars rover

F1 flag

Vintage car

ThrustSSC

Renault Clio

DeLorean DMC12

Rally car

Customized car

Car seat

Humvee

Six-wheel limousine

Smart car

Hot rod

MPV

Monster truck

Car tyre

Traffic light

Land Rover

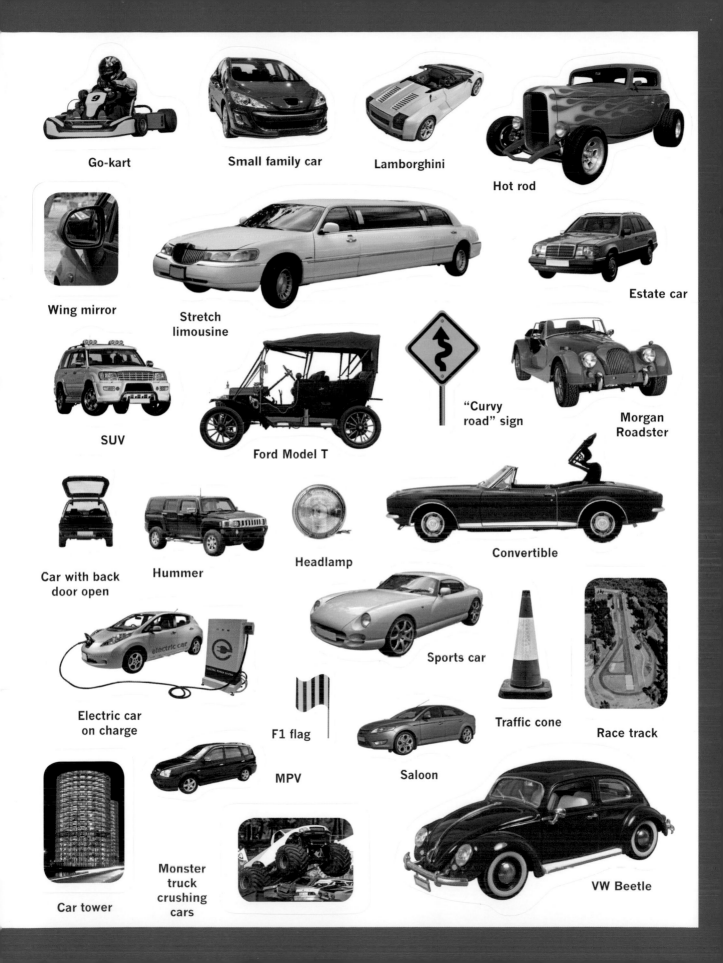

Go-kart

Small family car

Lamborghini

Hot rod

Wing mirror

Stretch limousine

Estate car

SUV

Ford Model T

"Curvy road" sign

Morgan Roadster

Car with back door open

Hummer

Headlamp

Convertible

Electric car on charge

Sports car

F1 flag

Traffic cone

Race track

MPV

Saloon

Car tower

Monster truck crushing cars

VW Beetle